Machine
Poems

Machine
Poems

Martin Hayes

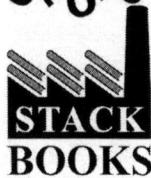

STACK
BOOKS

Smokestack Books
School Farm
Nether Silton
Thirsk
North Yorkshire
YO7 2JZ
e-mail: info@smokestack-books.co.uk
www.smokestack-books.co.uk

ISBN 9781738515417

Smokestack Books
is represented by
Inpress Ltd

for Fred –
a kindred spirit

'Robots are not sentient – they do not have the capacity to be coming for or stealing or killing or threatening to take away our jobs. Management do. Consulting firms and corporate leadership do. Entrepeners and tech execs do.'

Brian Merchant, *Blood in the Machine*

'The difference between technology and slavery is that slaves are fully aware that they are not free.

Nassim Nicholas Taleb

Contents

the definition of a machine

something that is made from following the instructions of a
blueprint
rather than the pure mistakes of lust
something that has been fashioned
with legs or arms that have been assembled
rather than grown
something that cannot learn but only repeat
something that can make or mend things
as easily as kill or break things
something whose mothers and fathers cannot be identified
apart from the manufacturer's tattoo on their skin
something that is not singular
but one of the many
something that doesn't eat
anything but electricity
that needs to be hooked up to some kind of power source
so it can reflect back its light into the people's faces
while they are sat in the dark
something so cunning so manipulative so addictive
it can turn you into one of them
without you even knowing it

our Serengetis

every morning at 5.30am
I leave my block
turn left
walk through the courtyard
go through the steel gate that creeks
like a tanker being let out to sea
and then I'm out
crossing the road
passing the ambulance station
where the paramedics are changing shifts
working out of the backs of their vans
in which they save lives in see hearts stop in
before going home to make breakfast for their children
and brush their teeth
then I'm down past the car wash
doing a right onto Edgware Road
past the tile shop the Persian restaurant
the Cypriot barbers that's been there for years
where I used to get my hair bowl-cut at 8
and then as I cross Frampton Street
slip in between the Transit vans parked up outside Embassy
    Plumbing
with the plumbers inside their cabins drinking tea or snoozing
waiting for Embassy Plumbing to open up
so they can get at the copper pipes and stopcocks they need
for their day's graft
and then suddenly I'm on Edgware Road proper
amongst the discarded chicken boxes the discarded pizza boxes
the pitta breads naan breads chicken bones pizza crusts
mounds of rice
pigeons pecking at sick pats chucked up the night before
and ahead of me is the Marylebone Rd flyover
rising up out of the fumes and mist like our Kilimanjaro

our Mount Fuji
as I head towards there aware
with my ears pricked up listening out for any predators
that might want to get in the way of my progress
who might be hiding away in shop doorways
prone in the scrub
ready to break cover
and burst full pelt across the road at me
wanting to sink their teeth into my underbelly
as I head down the half-mile to the Marylebone Road
past Paddington Green nick
then across Marylebone Road to hook a right alongside the
    Hilton Metropole
and as I wait by the bus stop there for the number 18
I watch the kerfuffle outside the hotel's staff door
it is like a watering hole
they all gather here
the cleaners the chambermaids the porters the dishwashers
the receptionists the handymen the waiters and waitresses
all smoking cigarettes before they go into work
or whenever they have a break
all holding plastic cups of coffee or tea in their hands
talking to each other
the men with Slav tongues unleashing words out of their mouths
like shells leaving a big ship's gun
quickly leaving the hot breath and smoke behind
before exploding in the air
and the ladies
letting their words exit their mouths like chucked knives
clashing and sharpening their metals
carving the air up into little bits
and the Africans there
all talking over-loudly and excitedly
like they've just won some kind of bet
spinning around while dragging deep down on their cigarettes
before throwing back their heads
and laughing that smoke out of their mouths

up into the cold air
then when the bus comes
I get on with the Somalians the Eritreans the Jamaicans
the Guyanese the Moroccans and the Slavs
all huddled up in their little bundles
tapping away at their phones or sleeping
as we all head in on the bus
pack together safe
passed the Travis Perkins by the roundabout
before coming up alongside the smart new offices of
    Paddington Basin
where a youth club once used to stand
where men once earned enough money
heaping sacks into the backs of barges and trucks and trains
that they could feed their families with it
which I now stare in at
from the top deck
to see an empty call centre
scores of annexed offices
with their whiteboards and giant flip-pads
where employees will later be taught
the intricate ways in which they have to perform
if they want to eat
if they want to keep a roof over their heads
as we go down under the underpass
and then up onto Harrow Road
up over the canal
passed the college
passed the shut-down stripper pub
the lawyer's offices offering benefit representation
the Westminster registration office
the giant Iceland
Shoe-Zone Angela's Nails the Bangladesh Caterers Association
the scores of ethnic supermarkets and chicken shops
Halal-Aldi Wingin' It
until my junction comes up
where I get off and walk up the last hill left

hook a left
and follow the bridge up over that dirty canal again
as on my left the sun rises up behind Trellic Tower
spreading its great oranges and purples across our great
unforgiving concrete savanna
before turning left into the road
that leads me finally down into work

the monarch butterfly does this
the blue whale does it
salmon
and wildebeest do it too
but they only do it once every year
while we do it every day
day after day
week after week
year after year
but no one ever makes documentaries about us
no one ever sits in front of their tellies of a night
listening to David Attenborough
tell us how beautiful it all is
that a man can travel the same path
every day
twice!
just so he can keep hold of his job
just so he can eat
drink
secure a mate

just so he is able
to carry on
surviving

just so he is able
to keep on
keeping on

Bear

it rained on that visit to the zoo
not normal rain
but as though the gates of some mythical flooded place
had opened up to scare away the packs and lonely souls
locked up in this brute establishment
it was empty
and I'd almost given up heading towards the exit
when I turned a corner
and there it was
a bear
9 foot high stood up on its hind legs
licking at the rain that caught then dripped
from the steel net above the bars of its cage
that kept in its incredible bulk
sinew moving muscle over bone an inch under its fur
that ridges of new continents could've be made from
if only there weren't more important things to contemplate
glimpsing then the flashes of its two-inch long white teeth
thick and strong as another animal's legs
that if you could trace back their roots
would be firmly embedded in the dark of the earth
where the fairies attend to the magical fires
and then that tongue of it
big and leathery and slithery
slippery and steaming and supple enough
able to turn in on itself
creating a shoot for the rain to ride down
before being swallowed by all of it
falling down then through its cavernous body
till it hit the floor of its stomach
some say it takes 10 days of falling
before anything reaches the floor of the stomach of a bear
and all the while clocking me as I came more into view

with those pin-hole miserable eyes set in the immensity of it
wondering almost looking sorry for me
that I was the one unfortunate enough
to have been born and locked in this human cage
and then when I got closer
pushing itself back down away from me
turning its planet as it went
to land it gracefully perfectly peacefully
to face the opposite direction of me
showing me then its big flanks
the mechanisms of its brute force buried deep inside its hips
before slowly strolling back into its manufactured den
to dream again
unimpressed with the sympathy on my face
when there's so much more still left inside to fight for

Hunger Games

over the kind earth the kind people walk
dumb as a thumb
without the rest of it attached
with strings connected to arms
with wooden brains and marbles for eyes
a moral compass like that of a chameleon-shaped windsock
a plate of last night's spaghetti
congealed through them as like a nervous system
heaving themselves
from one experiment to another
from one orgasm to another orgasm
from one history lesson to another history lesson

finally
exhausted
they return to their boxes
flop into their tissue paper armchairs
to sit in front of the news
watching the skill and wizardry of scientists
drop their dreams from the sky
exploding apart the atomic construction of a grandmother's heart
the binding tendons of a shopping mall
the pumping womb of a maternity hospital
the surprised face of a child
holding everything left it has
in a pink hippopotamus rucksack

shedding before bed
the next tear of their ascendancy
from the swamps and the seas

riding home with the precariat on a packed Bakerloo line again

call them ugly if you want
no man or woman that has ever shared their bed
would deny it
and no God
while they were before them on bended knee
has not fought back the urge
to slap them across the back of the head
or grant them everything, only in opposite, to their lame prayer

which nevertheless
either in misplaced belief or some substance ridden
keeps pouring out of their needy mouths
onto their bare but brightly lit dinner-table shore
only for when the scars and hunger get too pronounced to ignore
to be licked or stolen clean away
by their fit-for-the-coffin tongue
while gazing, always gazing
into the mists behind their shoulder
at their next unhealing wounds approaching

even to this day
I don't think they have properly loosened one inch
the chains and dreams that tie them
to their mysterious but battle-ready bed

the breast

there was this breast
and on the end of it
there was this copper nipple
and when they sucked on it
instead of milk it fed them money
and the more they sucked on it the fatter they got
but it was all they ever wanted
so they all went around looking for that breast
to latch onto
and it was good when they were on it
but bad when they were not
and sometimes while sucking away
they'd look up at what was above
and the owner of that breast wasn't their mother
but this big metal thing with eyes lit up red with fire
instead of eyelashes it had antenna
instead of nostrils it had two big chimneys chugging out smoke
instead of a mouth it had this opening
in which a furnace raged
eating everything up with its fire
so it could keep on producing money instead of milk
and it was as though their hunger would never diminish
and it was as though its fires would never stop
with the only answer seeming to be to cease feeding
if only for 5 minutes
to see if its fires would stop
which was impossible for the strong
but even harder for the weak
who were always only ever one or two feedings away
from disaster

here it was

a functional council block
not yet been allowed to slip
beyond repair to raze
gas and electricity still entered it
water still got hot to come out of its taps
and inside the people sat
watching TV or fussing over nothing
then when one of them died their unit was sold
then when another one died
that unit was sold
and this went on until there were only three left
who had the same purple doors
until in the end
those three became two
and both of them
the machine had its eye on
changing the text in the rules
so that when one of them died
there'd be only one
then when that one died
there'd be none
and it wouldn't be a council block anymore
but something else
like a very expensive tree
whose roots had been allowed to die
only for new ones to take their place
once every 6 months to a year

a healthy return

there was this place
it wasn't a town or a city
but people lived there
there was one shop and one pub
they all went to
and the shop had eggs and beans for the people to buy
but the shop shut down when the distribution company
couldn't get the eggs and beans to them
without a healthy return
then the busses that came through that place
twice back and forth everyday
also stopped coming
because there was no healthy return in it
then the people got sick
because they couldn't get to the doctor or the dentist
or the one library left or the one swimming pool left
until near the end
there was only the people left
in this place
and the pub
to which they all went
to drink the landlord's homemade gin
to talk about how they had all been
forgotten by the machine
until they all died out
and nothing existed anymore
in that place
or any of the other places
other than the rumour
that there'd been a people who once used to live around here
but they'd all died out
because there was no healthy return
to be had from any of them

what was said

the last people said
OMG these plastic implements we have to put around our noses
and mouths to breathe

and the ones before them said
let us live then
underground

and the ones before them said
look
up at the sky
it is browner than they predicted

and the ones before them said
ecology ecology
and they stood in the middle of roads
with their guts and fists out
trying to glue themselves into a barricade

and the ones before them said
I will go to Aldermaston and
I will not leave until all of their missiles
are disarmed

and the ones before them said
who shot Kennedy?

and the ones before them said
burn the bitch
she's a fucking witch

and the ones before them said
watch the stars

the way they turn and position themselves in the sky
it is the key

and the ones before them said
if it moves stab it kill it eat it
then bring its damp blood in buckets
so that we can ink it into our walls

and the ones before them said
from where did this machine come
to land here amongst such beasts

another timeline

they gave us the wheel
to start us off on the journey
then they gave us the forked road
so we could create the blues
pretend that we were able to make a choice

they gave us the octopus
to confuse and dumbfound us
and the dog
to see if it was *it* that we cherished
rather than what *it* could make us become

then they gave us the electricity pole and the flag
that we could separate ourselves
and begin on the road to our wars

then the machines came in their billions
each one switched on by a hand

and gradually, gradually...

they gave us the cup filled with oil
to celebrate their blood

they gave us the memory disc
to celebrate their flesh

they gave us the microchip
the tiniest biggest thing there ever was
to celebrate their hearts

and then they gave us their devices connected to the sky
made from the earth we'd left behind

then they gave us the abstractions
the apps the platforms the subscriptions the smiley faces
that we could lose the need for each other's warmth

and gradually, gradually...

we could see nothing that was behind us
with the only thing in front of us
what looked like to be our own hands
flailing about like two futuristic grabbing and crushing machines
    amongst the chaos and dust

the field

there was this field they called an office
where these creatures they called people
would come every day on buses or through the tube system
to sit in it
they were given computers to stare at instead of buttercups
and they were evaluated constantly
using the peas they produced placed against the peas they cost
and every day wasn't like a walk in the park
but more like a giant chess game
with strategy and sacrifice and ruthlessness in the air
and there was no sunlight that could reach in there
but it was all lit up with electricity
and it was hot every day
even in winter
and there was this thing
almost indistinguishable from a machine
that they called a supervisor
who patrolled the edges of the field
making sure there were no gaps in the fences
that kept the creatures in
in case they tried to escape

and this went on in every building in every city across the globe
while the machines and their peas reigned

falling in love with a machine

he said
I want to sit with you in a pub and drink with you
she said
I want to cannibalise you
he said
can't we just eat Thai food together
she said
I want to grate you like a piece of ginger over my metals
he said
I want to walk hand in hand with you along the Thames
she said
I want your seed inside me so that I can bake it into a little
miracle
he said
I am a man, I am Spartacus
she said
I will take you to the bed and destroy you
he said
you can't destroy what's not left
she said
I will find something in you, and when I do, I will concentrate
on that
he said
you scare me
she said
that's good, it's the beginning of what you call love
he said
how do you know that I won't run away and find another
she said
because you said you were Spartacus
and Spartacus's never run away

he said
okay, you've got me there
she said
well let's get on with it then

food for the hideous Sun

there was this time
way before men and women lived
when hearts were being prepared
before being handed out to them

it wasn't in a womb or a wood or a forest this happened
it was in the rings around Saturn
and when they were ready
Saturn chucked them off to Earth with every spin

some of the hearts misjudged
the exact angle and point of penetration
into the Earth's atmosphere needed
and so careered off towards the Sun
65 million years later becoming what we now call solar flares

others
too stupid or insensitive to be dissolved by fire
got through all on their own
and that's why we've had Hitler's Mussolini's Netanyahu's and
    Thatcher's

others on the other hand
fearing coming to the entry point all on their own
used to grip a hand 4 million miles out
then on the journey in
tried to glide and time their entry point together
at exactly the right place at exactly the right angle
and side by side
it was learnt that two of them had more chance of surviving

than one
and that's why humans fall in love
forge lifelong friendships
believe in fairy tales
or have an inexplicable solidarity with things that are now almost
    gone
because if you don't have at least two hearts fighting together
you'd be nothing

other than food for the hideous Sun

the last unclassifiable thing left in the world

its threadbare gene lays down
on the glass slide
drugged to the hilt

the plasticised hands slowly push a needle into it
drawing back
fluid

surprised
it hasn't already given up its secret
they put what's left of it in a jar
shake it
freeze it
defrost it
freeze it again
then they shine a light into where they think it has an eye
bash it with a number
over where they think it has a head
bombard it with electromagnetic beams
in the hope that it will radiate
and light up the way

after their surprise
that this one isn't buckling
turns to consternation
they run it through a billion-pound machine
at close to the speed of light
until it feels so dizzy
it thinks that it is in a cave
in the centre of a mountain
falling off the edge of the world
(that's why lovers tend to hold hands)

then before it has recovered from that
they stretch it
shrink it
sing lullabies to it
all in the hope that it will either cry
or at least move again

then they give it a name
like they give a hurricane a name

then they try to predict it
what it will do next
placed under such scrutiny

this will go on for as long as the grant money exists
or until something else is discovered
that hasn't been discovered yet

or until one of them eventually shouts

'look! look!
I think I have found something!'

then everyone will come rushing over
and they will all gather
as though in a huddle
over some old leather-bound book

their bright clean instruments
that some of us call hearts
pumping uncontrollably

and after it looks like it can be nothing else
they will all throw their heads up
and in unison
scream

'YES! YES!
IT IS A FACT!
LOVE IS DEAD!'

despite this though
girls and boys will still fall head over heels into it
and sometimes
they will even do it in the rain

the mule

she asks we why I can't write
on a Monday night or a Tuesday night a Wednesday or a
    Thursday night
why does it always have to be on a Friday night
that spills over into our Saturdays

I tell her that it was a Friday night
when Hemingway caught the big fish
it was when Neruda decided that he had to run over the
    mountains on a mule
to save his life
it was the night when Guy Fawkes poured all of that gunpowder
    into his bombs
when Zurita decided to tip acid into his eyes on those steps
because he couldn't take seeing what was being done to his
    people anymore

she says nights are just nights
what's the bloody difference

I tell her that I don't know why either
Friday nights just feel different
that they are special
maybe it's the psychological snap at the end of a working week
when the bridge that crosses the ravine
suddenly collapses
with all of them on one side
and all of us left feeling freer on the other
I don't know ·
but things rise up out of the ground on a Friday night
and wave all of their blood around
like in voodoo or tarot
there's a certain kind of magic in the air

that you've got to latch on to
or else what's the point
of even being alive man

she is not a believer though
says that Gogglebox is on on a Friday night
and you just ruin it
doing all of your writing stuff and dancing around
singing out
with your headphones on

we will work it out
I am not Hemingway Neruda Guy Fawkes or Zurita
but she is my lady
and even though she doesn't believe or even know it
she is the one who carries me over the mountains
who pours the gunpowder into me with her hooves

another offering

the two of them sat
on a maternity ward
holding hands
for three days
she was having trouble
so they stuck a needle in her back
one of the midwives was from New Zealand
wore bright white trainers
with little gold coconuts printed all over them
the other one was from Liberia
wore Crocs and had two big swimming pool eyes
told us that babies were like raindrops
that they all drop from the sky
once they get too heavy for the clouds to hold
it came out in the end
was a girl
no one knew what she might become
the machine was waiting
with its mouth open

growing up

it was before
the child hadn't yet got his job
when the mother asked him
when is it you're going out into the world son?
the world? the child asked, what is that?
it's where I'm not the mother, the mother said
where the machines rattle and clatter and instead of wind passing
    through the trees
their metal teeth will
and you'll be one of the leaves
I'm not sure I like the sound of that, the child said
it's unavoidable, the mother said, as she went around
    dismantling his bed
so the child put his boots on and stepped out the door
immediately the wind took him up into the sky and dropped him
    off behind a counter at Greggs
then at Kwik Fit levering tyres off and replacing them with new ones
then at night in the new job on the outskirts of the city
where the owls sat in their high corners searching with their
    big radars
the field beside the warehouse where the child's pallets needed to
    be stacked
it all started to make sense
and it was around this time
the child started knowing that nothing happens without him
that the splinters and callouses on his hands
were the real beginning

Christmas time the child came back, exhausted
and the mother said, see, the world is big, isn't it?

bread and circuses

here they come again
on a rainy Monday morning
into the tube system
then all the other days
with their tired faces on
last night's TV already forgotten
and a belly full of cheap fried chicken

they say
getting fed and constantly entertained
can keep a misused dog quiet for long enough
that it forgets the things it once used to bark at

tired now from their dealings with supervisors
they accept their pay
all have at least two TV controls on the arms of their chairs
all of them?
Yes! and apps on their phones
that can bring to their doors
curries noodles burgers and chips
and crispy duck-filled buns

it is difficult to stay angry
on a full belly
a mind constantly drowned under a sea of irrelevance
all of the noise in the blood gets turned down
chloroformed by the salt and sugar
and indifferent about it
they wander around
unsure of what's expected of them
living life as life
rather than as metaphor

where the sun shines black and the stars never move

they put up with the alarm clock
the bleeding gums
the price of a coffee
the oppressiveness
of feeling like cattle
while moving through the tube system

then once in
they put up with the inadequate software
the tin-pot hardware
the client's rudeness the courier's rage
they put up with last minute changes of shift patterns
the snide comments of supervisors
letting them know that they are
considered an idiot
in meetings in which they are told
that they have to do more

and on the way home
they put up with the tiredness the monotony
the numbness the uselessness
of a sky in which the sun shines black
and the stars never move

because it was the only freedom they knew

tomorrow

tomorrow he will look after his liver
tomorrow he will get his hair cut
tomorrow he will sign off in his head
the purchasing of a Nutribullit
and blitz before he goes to bed
a green magic drink full of avocados apples and kale
so that he can then start the process
of signing off the purchasing of a suit
so that he can look like the rest of them in the office
tomorrow he will stop smoking
and start to make amends with his lungs
tomorrow he will run a bath
fill it with bubbles scented with lemongrass
ease himself into it surrounded by candles
so that he can start giving back to his body what it has given to him
tomorrow he will get off the tube at Aldgate
and walk the mile up to work in Whitechapel
so that his heart gets some different work inside it
other than this pain
tomorrow as he lays in his bed trying to sleep
he will tell himself to try and remember the dreams
so that they might come back to him when he is awake
tomorrow he will cease looking down
give up the fight
of rummaging through all of the old rubbish
for remnants of the past
and look up at the new sun
rising like a furnace out of everyone's mouths
lighting up the machines of the future

tomorrow he will do it

he will do it

tonight though
he will drink at the typer
and look after his soul
in case it feels that it has been abandoned
when tomorrow comes

work

it is constant
it walks beside you
when you should've left it behind

it sits next to you on the tube
holds your hand
speaks into your ear
about the things you should've done
the things
you shouldn't have done

along the Edgware Rd up to home
it is behind you
in front of you
circling around you
like a pack of hungry dogs
you
trying to keep your arse away
from its snapping jaws

inside you take off your boots
wash
switch on the telly
open a can of beer

it is still there
staring at you
wanting to know
this or that

there is no respite from it

it is the only thing that pays the rent

the food the electricity the toothpaste
the plasters Bonjela codeine and wine

without it
you are homeless
with it
you are a slave
and constantly
it reminds you of this

he is a building site

his two arms are cranes
his eyes
two red dots blinking away at the top of them
his shoulder-blades are the power source
they lift and turn his arms around
his fingertips
are buckets of cement
his arms drop them down onto their buttons

sometimes it rains there
thunderstorms and lightning seen from an 8th floor office
can make him feel like he's in the sky
being buffeted around like a lost plastic bag

the new girl Sarah
tells him that it reminds her of the time before the machines
when the fields her family used to farm up in Shropshire
got inundated with water
and no work could be done
until it all drained away

every spring
her fingers used to pull calves out of the wombs of ewes

her arms are becoming like cranes now
she still has two blue eyes
blinking away at the top of them
but they will be red within a month
the farm dead to insolvency
the father hung from the rafters of an out-barn
what else can you do
having to head for the city

turns your ribcage into scaffolding
your heart into a punch-press
all of your memories change
everything becomes steel

the machine virus

of course, there is just you bound to the machine virus
sat in this early morning office of cool slaughter
where the new buds come to grow their stern stems
to flower another flower that will not petal transformation
just more acceptance of the hot sun's rays
whose heat wilts an infant heart to its knees
guts can be bought for a pauper's sum per month
and silence for just a little bit more

of course, there are others bound to the machine virus
wracked in sweat unable to find the cipher
to unpick the chains of debt that clank and stoke their fever
no noise is good noise the bald ones say
as tongues get ripped from throats
to pile or hang upon their back walls like trophies
tunnelling is an old art
unlearned in these upright swamps of concrete and glass
that suffocate the din of man and woman's penniless rage

of course, we all lay bound to the machine virus
tied to weathers that grow their thorny arms
wrapping their lust for constant growth around us
locking us in to their unwinnable game
the wounds are felt by many
everything becomes heavy
the nicks and scars a reminder
some men and women have to get by on rage alone
while freedom still burns its question mark into their skin

you work next to men for years

you work next to men for years
gain ideas about how they tick
study their body language
the things that they say

you work next to men for years
as blood runs over the bone
as the dirty river outside
slowly slinks past

you work next to men for years
you watch them change
you watch them shrink
you watch them
slow
down
you watch them
become prey

and all you're left with
after the years have passed
after the time has been put in
is a vague sense
of waste
that you've all been used
that if you had your time over again
you would've collected more tunnelling implements
not borrowed so much money
surrounded yourself with more dogs
and walked out more over the moors
when the rain and lightning was coming in
just to see if you could've found something else
other than this feeling
of having been eaten by a machine

the dull fog

look at David, he's a controller
walking in with his too-long-under-the-iron polyester strides on
shining like a pair of legs wrapped up in cling film
with a shirt on the iron missed
at its collar and other bits
feet and stamina are his language
bombs of hope placed inside a pair of 99p socks -
some say you can find the insistence that God exists
in the quite times while walking in the mist and fog of the hills
when the heart pumps another clot out if it -
but the tube-map and pubs are David's fields to navigate
all of him pushed after the night before to get himself in
to sit in front of a screen that will throw its weathers at him
light rain at first but the wind will gather
the clouds on the borders of his territory
and unannounced sweep in
with their hail and flashes of lightning
all day he will try to avoid their calamity
trying to do his job balanced on the edge of panic and anxiety
muttering to himself the whole way home
about all the things he missed
back to his one room
above the supermarket
where no weathers form but for the dull fog

returning to Stockholm Street and Syndrome Way

he said he'd never come back
he said he'd never return
he said he didn't want
to be a part of the backstabbing anymore
he said he wanted no part
in the snide comments
the fear the betrayal the sense of
worthlessness
that the supervisors got to hang around our necks
like they were our keepers
he said he was sick
of the constant anxiety
working under a regime whose system
promoted torture and humiliation
he said his mental health was deteriorating
that he had to get away
that the good times
the buzz the excitement
the juggling of all those balls
the finding of the couriers out there trying to earn their money
against the covering of all those jobs
the intensity of it all
all those equations
and that rocket-engine roar that'd erupt inside him
whenever it started to get busy
the way everything seemed to lift up off the floor
like it was all now on a magic carpet
that's what he'd miss
he said the camaraderie and purchase of that
making it feel more than just a job
were the things he'd have to forgo
before he did something stupid to himself

he returned last Thursday
came back
said the new job he'd gone to
had left him bored shitless
with no excitement no enthusiasm
working from home 3 days a week on his own
isolated lonely singular
it was killing him
was slowly turning him into a machine
he had to leave
before he did something stupid to himself

he's sitting at his old desk now
in the control room
across the way from me
right on the corner of Stockholm Street
and Syndrome Way

the wisdom of dung beetles

whenever the operating system at your workstation develops a fault
you have to fill out a R145 form
and send it off to the IT department on an email
if the fault means you can't access your emails
then you have to contact your line manager and tell him about it
he will then follow you back to your workstation
brushing aside everything you try to tell him on the way
before pulling out your monitor turning it on its side
checking that all the cables are tight in their sockets
and haven't come loose
if that doesn't work
he'll get down on his hands and knees
and pull the pc box out from under your desk
unplugging cables then plugging them back in again
then if that doesn't work
he'll leave your workstation in a mess
and walk away saying that he has a meeting to attend
we can't walk up to the IT department and speak to them
because the IT department is outsourced
and resides in a building or cloud either in Peterborough or above
    Shanghai
it's not been discovered where yet
so you sit
amongst the mess of your workstation
waiting thinking about goats on the side of a hill eating grass
then you think that you can use the 4G on your phone
to send the R145 form to the IT department
so you do that and within seconds you get back a response
saying that this isn't a company registered email address
that you should contact your line manager
for further support
so you sit there again
waiting thinking about how beautiful Helen must've been

that thousands of men were sent out to war over her
then finally
your line manager will return from his meeting
telling you that he's got hold of IT
and that their advice
is to switch it off
then turn it back on again
as you sit there thinking
about the wisdom of dung beetles
rolling all of those little balls of shit around
just so they can make a home

limbs and blood

it was 6.30 am
he was already there when I got in
inside the driver room waiting for me
I dumped my stuff off and went in to see him
his world was caving in
his wife was living in Kingston he was living in Uxbridge
the two kids were still living in Streatham because of their schools
how? I asked
he showed me the bailiff notice so I could see how
and also the cost of running the bike
with courier insurance tyres petrol servicing to keep it legal
he laid out all of the bills on the table
all crumpled up looking like tinder that could start a big bonfire
and the food and the rent and the heat
I thought losing my left leg up to my knee in the accident was hard
but this is something else he said
I was on one side of the desk and he was on the other
his eyes started to bulge and began to water
all of it had come to Marcelo's singularity and was about to explode
there was nothing I could do to help
but increase his hourly rate from £12 to something more he said
something extra
so that he could stop everything for a bit
and start putting it all back together

I said I'd speak with the people who had the say
asked him again
if there was anything else I could do to help
he said no
just the money
you get that right then I can start reversing everything
begin trying to put it all back together

I knew it was going to be difficult
to convince them
because the machine thinks in numbers you see
rather than in limbs and blood

the other war

Dalila, Delta 4-3-2, Brazilian/Portuguese with a mane of blonde hair
shot through with dark brown
came in last Thursday wanting to talk to somebody about her money
in the kitchen I offered her tea or coffee
she took tea
after a minute of pleasantries she got down to her business
told me how her hourly rate wasn't enough to even keep her
motorbike on the road anymore
what with all the rising costs of fuel
tyres brake-pads servicing courier insurance
and then there was the home to look after
having to log on to the food-apps after finishing her 10 hours with us
for another 4 hours
finishing past 11 just to earn that little bit extra
to help pay a bit more towards the rent
a bit more towards the council tax
a bit more towards the energy company's ransom
and don't even talk to her about the kids or a social life
she hasn't been out for 8 months
the two kids continually bombarding her
wanting all of the latest devices phone contracts
money to go out
everything was like a war now she said
with the only weapon needed as a deterrent
to her and her family's total annihilation
more of the machine's money

I knew that the people who had the final say wouldn't understand
would say something like
well if she doesn't like it then replace her
there's tons of them out there all crawling over each other to get at
    £12 per hour

your too soft
tell her to fuck off
but instead I told her that I would take her case to them
she said thank you
I said would you like more tea
she said no
just more money please
then she got up
took her mane of blonde hair shot through with dark brown
and went out there to do it all over again

run

you gotta run
you gotta leave it all behind
you gotta find the idea
that train
that will take your body away
the soul within will remain
you will remain
but you gotta run

not running
is an acceptance of everything
as it is
it will stop you from thinking
about bumblebees
acorns
the power a cat has
able to live on its own
amongst the tall grass

it will stop you from laughing
at yourself
it will stop you from loving
toenails
fish
butterflies
custard
and rain

you gotta run
or they will tie you up in knots
to their posts
in rope
in black satin ribbon
stand you in quicksand
then abandon you

you gotta run
now!
before it's too late
before their cement thickens
before they snuff out your fire
before you lose the urge the urgency
that you need to run
before you forget
that running was even an option
in the first place

water ghosts and dragons

for Zheng Xiaoqiong

I work in a clothing factory in Guangzhou
the cotton comes at night in big trucks from somewhere behind
    the mountains
the noise they make unloading the cotton stops me sleeping
when I can't sleep
I think of my younger brother in a pond back home when a frog
    jumped on his shoulder
my older sister at school getting bullied
my mother going there on the warpath
when she was still alive rather than now dead from stomach cancer
when the cotton is made into garments in the Big Place
they come to us on a conveyor belt like the cold wind comes in
    October
we must stamp on them the slogans of the West
Champion, Nike, Slazenger, M&S –
the machines that house these stabbing programmes are made of
    steel
we must pull the garments inside out
position them under the machine, press a green button
so that they can start stabbing the cotton in
we watch them do their magic
we hold in our hands the garment afterwards
wonder who will wear this one in the West
I guess we are like machines also now
we guide the material underneath the stabbing machines
let the needles and thread follow the programme to do the rest
they are not like the old witches, our grandmothers from the past
who used to knit our initials into our socks with their hands
pulling them over our feet while telling us stories about water
    ghosts and dragons
before letting us fall asleep in their arms

we are different to that now
we must make sure the logos get set and woven
so people in the West can feel cool
the programme in the steel machines is good
it makes very few mistakes
the machine is more powerful now
than many of our memories
it pays us to forget

under the iron moon

Gong Zonghui female 20 years old
lost 4 fingers after losing control of an industrial punch press
the callouses and blisters on her hands
were in their 14th hour
of a double shift
people reported that she didn't cry
she didn't scream
she just grabbed up her fingers
and walked off

Tang Yihong had been away in the city for so long
when he returned home
his young son didn't recognise him
stood behind his mother's body like it were a shield
whose eyes saw a different man
walk out of the storm

Xu Lizhi walked to the top of his dormitory building
threw himself off its edge
though his colleagues had seen it coming
no witnesses saw it happen
apart from the iron moon

they leave when they are young
for the City of Chances
their hearts left behind under their beds
in the hope that they won't have anything left
in which to carry the pain around with

but what can we do or care
the moon is a different witness over there
by the time it has been shipped over to us
the clouds have wiped the evidence
clean from its face

let's have more poets like Xu Lizhi

let's have more poets like Xu Lizhi
let's have more of their iron exposed
writing about the fella in Dormitory 2
who opened his belly to the iron moon
with a rusty knife

let's have more poets like Zheng Xiaoqiong
writing about the woman she slept next to in Dormitory 6
who carved an X into her breast
every month she couldn't send money back to her family in
    Sichuan Province

let's have more poets
who have lived and seen things
let's have more poets
who want to speak above the din of the machines
let them
drown out these non-poets with non-sentences that non-resonate

let's have more poets
who carry their hands home with them
with fingers missing
let's have more poets
rooted into the red earth
with more guts rather than more words

let's have more poets like that!

not poets who turn a blind eye
pretending to be unwed to these machines
not poets who want to drown us
with their beautiful words

please
let us have more poets
with if not fingers missing
then something else that separates them
from the very damaged worn down utterly exhausted water nymph

we don't need any more exhausted water nymphs
in Dormitory 8
there are real people
with a left arm missing
and both legs torn from the knee down

let us have more poets like Xu Lizhi
please
let us have more of them
the world needs them

all we need to know

in which the word cable has been replaced by the word poetry

when the Titanic sank
the *Mackay-Bennet,* a *poetry* laying ship, was sent from Halifax
   Nova Scotia
loaded with embalming supplies, a hundred coffins and two
   hundred tons of ice
to recover the drowned
when it arrived
there were hundreds of bodies floating about in the sea
and it soon became obvious
that there were too many bodies for the ship to hold
the system was brutal, but it went like this:
those that could be identified as 1st class passengers
were carefully embalmed and put in coffins
before being stored in the *poetry* hold
those identified as 2nd class passengers
were wrapped in linen winding sheets
and placed in the Forward and middle-class *poetry* lockers
where the two hundred tons of ice had been previously stored
and those identified as 3rd class passengers
or who were unable to be identified
by the strict rules now in place
because identity and division had become paramount
were weighted and slipped back into the sea

the silencing

it was in the little bits of space/time
in between him being used and not used
that he heard it
and having known nothing
before but the machine's clunks and clicks and swipes
he said
What is this? Where does it come from?
then he memorised it
and stuck it in his left ear
amongst the hairs that guarded
the opening into the sea of his head
and he wrote poems about it for three decades
before the machine finally found it and took it
to its HR department at the top of the hill above the city
and decapitated it

diversify or die

The man in the corner shop said yes
Of course I need to diversify
I can't keep going on selling only these newspapers and crisps
Because I will die

The butcher said yes
Of course I need to diversify
I can't keep going on selling only these raw cuts of meat
Because I will die

The owner of the factory said yes
Of course I need to diversify
I can't keep going on making only these plastic buttons
Because I will die

And the owner of the other factory said
I too need to diversify
Because if I keep going on making only these steel hinges
I will die

And then the poet said, shit
I guess I'm going to have to diversify too
Because if I keep going on writing only these poems about work
I'm going to die as well

As underneath the earth the machine started to break free from
its chains
And a big roar, like no other roar ever heard or imagined, began
to exit from its throat

openings

when they noticed
a gap in the fence
that worked perfectly fine
letting the creatures in and out as they pleased
they gave us the electric current
its ability to run through yards of barbed wire

when they noticed a doorway that had a door
without a lock on it
so that the creatures could freely walk
from one office to another office
from one part of the building to another part of the building
or from one part of the Earth to another part of the Earth
they gave us the key and fob system
so that everything could be regulated and contained

when they noticed a crack in the wall
wide enough for when the creatures were to turn their bodies
    sideways
they could slip through it
transfer themselves from one side to the other
they gave us their devices
to distract us all
as they hurriedly went around
trying to fill them all in

and when they noticed
that sometimes the creatures mouths wouldn't open
when questioned about those who'd managed to circumnavigate
    their artifices
even when tortured and threatened with the worst
they gave us the electric baton and a pair of pliers

in fact
whenever they noticed anything associated with any kind of
    opening
they sent or gave us something
that wanted to control
what came in
or what came out of it

more magical and beautiful than any machine

I don't know whether it was a gyroscope a radar
or some other similar technology
that Marcus had in his head
but whenever he sat down at the control point on a busy Friday
    afternoon
to allocate the jobs to couriers
rather than the 30 minutes it took us other controllers
to work out where all the couriers were
he seemed to know where they were instantly
then whoosh!
his fingers began to dance over his keypad like dragonflies
allocating out jobs to the correct couriers
so that the screens momentarily began to clear
and it was like some mystical event was taking place in front of us
that we'd only heard or read about before in the bible
or now see in CGI films
and when the next wave of jobs started to come in
dropping down onto his screen like confetti
he'd position himself on the edge of his seat
with his spine perfectly straight
half-in half-out of something
jabbering away into his mic instructions to the couriers
to drop this one first
to keep hold of that one and collect this one first
and again
he managed to push back the torrent before it flooded us all
and for all us other controllers
it was like being in the presence of a Da Vinci
or being in the front row seats
when Ali (art) took down Foreman (strength)
or witnessing live
that moment when Marilyn Monroe's white chiffon dress
got blown up by the wind coming out of those subway grates

then when it got to around 4 pm
and there was no chance anymore
of another torrent of jobs coming in
he'd get up from his controller's chair
and hand it over to another controller

people wonder if technology or some other AI
will eventually replace us humans
to do the jobs and the art in the same way we can
and for most of the time
it probably will
but when it gets busy in a courier control room on a Friday
    afternoon
or something else rises that needs calling out
in a poem in a book in a song
some men and women
with the veins and blood and the heart pumping away inside them
are far more magical and beautiful than any machine

hired by a machine

the link is the first thing
do you just click on it?
do you right-click then search for where you open it?
or do you have to copy it then paste it into your browser?
is it an open-in-a-new-window one?
or will it just appear on the screen
overwriting all else before?
will the back-button work?

then once you're in
you begin to wander around their labyrinth
searching for the right part
then after you've found it
you click on the application part of it
and begin

two hours later
after one hundred and twenty four questions
and the uploading of seven id documents
you are told by the screen
that you'll hear back within 24 hours

overnight it came in
at 3.16am
when nothing is awake apart from the drunks and the stars
an email saying that you've been successful at the first stage
are now invited to an orientation session
that you have to attend online
within seventy-two hours of receiving this email
to click on the link below
to start your tour
whenever ready
making sure you had 90 minutes spare

because there'd be a test at the end
followed quickly by the decision
whether you'd got the job or not

he couldn't bring himself to do it
he'd lost all heart
if you can pass the interview process
get invited to view the company's ways of work
only for soon after that
to potentially be given an actual job
without seeing or speaking to one single person
you can sort of guess
what sort of people work there
that they don't value very much
eyes
or anything else for that matter
that goes to make up a human being
never mind a whole workforce of them

don't try

you don't have to do anything
you don't have to try
the more you try
the more you'll get entrapped
let the bluebells grow
let the weeds grow
let the cold get in
let the damp rise

don't believe
you can't change anything
by doing nothing
history is filled with people
who have tried to change the world
by doing something

yet here we still are

save your energy for drinking
eating
kissing
and holding hands with the one you love most

nothing else matters

you don't have to do anything
you don't have to try
trying will just make you more confused
trying to be the best will leave you drained
more upset
than if you hadn't tried
in the first place
you don't have to try

not trying
not needing to do it
it will get you into what's inside your ribcage
swans
moonlight
the architecture of toes
and wine

not trying
you'll end up understanding why dragonflies only live for 7 days
why some monkeys try to kill themselves when placed in
captivity
why whales dive into the deep ocean
only to sing to themselves
about nothing anybody understands
other than other whales

don't try
don't do anything
others have done it before
you are not the first one

and when you lift a glass of red up to your lips on a Friday night
after work
not trying
will hopefully let you understand
that you don't have to do anything
be anything
and the more you do it
the more you will enjoy
this pain of being alive

others have done it before
you are not the first one
but when you do it
if you can
it will feel like you are

the machine sends in some help

Constantine is fresh in off the HR Express
she wears a grey suit with a white blouse and carries a reusable cup
sipping at the artisan coffee inside it almost constantly
Constantine wants to know everything
she wants to get under the skin of the company's culture
so that she can better deal with anything that lands on her desk
Constantine takes her job seriously
she comes out of her glass office next to the CEO's
and walks around the control room on a busy Friday afternoon
asking us questions
as she does this she is asked by Antoine whether she would like to
come out on a date with him
met
by Ronnie's lonely head that's fallen back on its neck again
with his eyes pointing straight up into the ceiling
while his hands and fingertips keep tapping away at his keypad
as though he has two parts to him
by Ben
who has just come out of the toilet after visiting his
uncle Charlie again
wanting to know where she comes from, what area?what music do
you like?what food do you prefer? you seen *Apocalypse Now*?
Natural Born Killers?
sounding her out like a sonar beam made up of chemicals rather
than light
by Matthew
who has a blister forming on his cheek set in amongst all
the eczema
who straight up asks her if she is gonna be able to do something
about his overtime rate
the chaotic shift-patterns he keeps getting assigned
by Leon
who asks her if she has any advice he can use

trying to square the circle with his wife back home
who's got him sleeping on the couch now
because he hasn't yet been able to give her a house with a garden
and a tree she can sit under
so she can forget about Leon
and by Marcus
who is slaughtered with all of the jobs coming in
dropping down onto his screen like confetti
asking her whether she knows anybody with an almost
passable passport
that would be willing to come and jump into one of our vans
to try and help us out of this mess

Constantine might come and save somebody one day
but not those who work at Phoenix Express
not right here
not right now

the camouflage of dragons

I used to think that dragons didn't exist
that they were things made up for the telly or to bring myths
alive
but when Constantine came to head up our HR department
walking around the control room her first week
asking us questions about why we did this why we did that
you could feel a warmth coming off her that wasn't natural
she was so nice
like your nan
only in a 32-year-old body
who wanted to make sure you got your tea on time
then in her 2nd week she made us all origami dragons
and placed them on the keypads at our control points
before we came in
then in her 3rd week she didn't come into the control room so
much
to ask us how things were going
instead, she was moved into the glass office next to the CEO's
and we could all see her in there typing away at her computer
until all the glass started to steam up from the heat she gave off
we thought she was drafting up our new contracts
in which we would get sick-pay and time-and-a-half for
overtime
that she was dealing with the small print
so that it would protect us from the supervisor's hideous moods
which much like the weather
would batter its winds and hail against us one day
only to bathe us in glorious sunshine the next
then in her 4th week
she didn't come in at all
was off attending a course in Coventry
about how to glide safely through the grey areas of the sky
when it came to worker's rights in the workplace
then in her 5th week

the first rumours that Constantine was really a dragon started
because when Georgia came back from going to the loo
she told everyone that she'd seen this big reptile tail poking out
of one of the cubicles
and Constantine wasn't in her office
or on a course
then in her 6th week
Rushab, who did the 1pm to 11pm shift, said that when he was
leaving the building the night before
he heard this big whoosh pass over his head
like it was a giant bird swooping down trying to grab him up in
its claws
but Bart said to him that he was going mad
that it was most probably the air ambulance lifting off from
London Hospital again
but Rushab said no
I know a raptor from a helicopter
then in Constantine's 7th week 4 telephonists disappeared
then in her 8th week Maria the cleaner disappeared
only to be replaced by two men who wore Mitie badges on their
chests
then in her 9th week
she sent us all an e-card from the Maldives
that dropped into our inboxes at 11am on a busy Friday
morning
telling us how much she was thinking about us
and I think all of us went home that weekend
half-hoping for a hurricane or a tsunami
to target precisely that island resort she was on
but it wouldn't have mattered
it wouldn't have mattered even if an earthquake had opened up
and swallowed that resort whole
because dragons can lift off at a milliseconds notice
and stay airborne for years
carrying carrion in their claws
storing flesh in their oven throats
which is what they use to produce their fire

how to kill a cleaner

when Maria the cleaner was told by Constantine the HR manager
that her services wouldn't be needed after the end of the month
her bright blue eyes suddenly got bigger
and then when Maria asked Constantine why
Constantine said that it was just a change of focus the business was
going through
that hand-to-mouth agreements were not policy anymore
and contracted companies with clear health and safety policies
was where the business needed to go
if only to protect itself
Maria then got more upset, said, I am healthy and safe, I use gloves
every time on the desks
that's not what I mean, Constatine chuckled back
what is it you mean then, Maria asked, am I doing something wrong?
no, Constantine said, you have been a good servant to the company
for years
and we appreciate all of the effort you have put in
but the company is taking a new course now and needs to contract
things out
so that it can protect itself from risk
risk? risk? Maria said, you think I am a risk?
no, Constantine said, it's just that contracts protect businesses from
all sorts of things
I protect this business too, Maria said, I protect it from all sorts of
things
there's the dirt and dust I wipe away
I wipe up all their sticky Lucozade rings on their dirty desks
I wash all their cups they leave on the side by the kettle every night
I empty their bins pick chewing gum that they spit from their mouths
from the bottom of their bins
I do what is necessary in their toilets and clean the woman's bin of all
their blood
I make sure all the handles to all the doors are wiped so no germs

in the director's offices I turn their keypads over and bang them on
the desk
use a wipe to pick up all the skin cells and bogey stuff
so what do you mean when you say 'protect'?
Maria, Constantine said, it's not your performance or your abilities
that are in question here
the business is just moving in a different direction and your
services are not going to be needed anymore
why not, Maria said, you think there won't be any more sticky
circles or dust and bins to clean?
you think the shit and blood in the toilets is going to stop?
you think the directors will stop shedding their skin and sneezing
out their bogeys?
listen, Maria, Constantine said, I can tell you are getting a bit
agitated...
agitated, Maria went back, what is this agitated?
...look, Constantine said, I've tried to do this nicely
I know you've put a lot of effort in
worked hard cleaning the mess up that the controllers leave behind
but I'm telling you now
don't fuck with me okay
because those big eyes of yours mean nothing to me
and the reason I don't give a fuck
about your big eyes or anything else
is because I'm really a dragon...

then Constantine's desk began to rattle
and the whole office started to shake
then from underneath the table two big reptile wings
suddenly appeared
rose up into the air
and attached themselves to Constantine's shoulders
and before Maria could run to get out the door
fire came out of Constantine's mouth
and turned Maria to ash

thus proving
once again
that you can stand up as much as you like
for your job your family your existence
but if a dragon has its eye on you
then it won't be long before it will turn you into ash

the message

when you have lived with prophecy for so long
the moment of revelation is a shock
and though you shall know their ways
as though born to them
some things you work on tirelessly
will never be brought to harvest

they will want to drink a lot from you
eat too much of you
your misplaced tolerance and misplaced rage
will be their food

they will be silent for what seems like ages
but all the while they will be whispering into your ear
and if you work for them for long enough
inside one of their steel chapels
there will come a time
amongst the tall grass surrounding them
when you will finally hear it

you are mine!

you are mine!

how deadly is its poison

who made these overpopulated tubes
we must board each day just to get at our plunder
not the rank and file who in stupidity or lust
were lured from the lonely path through the tall grass
where the dogs play in peace and the bluebells grow in silence

only a machine could devise such routes and ways
for us to tread peacefully into existence
only to exit them, then wander in between their iron trees
to seek the office to do what we need to do with our hands
so we don't starve

and at the end of it
how deadly is its poison
that we must sit for 10 hours each day drinking it
for years
and then more years

the worker writer

what does he know
apart from the shrill bell of his alarm clock and the tube map
that gets him in to do their dirty work
there are no fields for him to saunter
or drag his limbs through their poetic mud
or regurgitate with crafted pen or plough
heaven's true story

his is more a theft from the earth than a sharing -
when you've been used for so long
it's not such a leap to become a user -
and no joy does he get from it either
other than paying the rent and showing
everyone
what he and his ilk are capable of

the people kept on yelling

the machine said, work
and the people said back
work, yes, but let it be fair!

and then the machine said,
shut up, just keep on working
and the people said back
work, yes, but let it be fair!

and then the machine sent its supervisors in
to slap them across the back of their legs
with a baton
but the people took it and said back
work, yes, but let it be fair!

and then the machine's supervisors said
Fair!? I'll show you what's fucking Fair!
and then they invented their HR department
to try and crush every uprising with its rules
but the people kept on yelling
work, yes, but let it be fair!

and the moon kept on coming and going
and the sea was always there
and nothing could kill what was in the core of the people
which was work and love
and the machine understood this
so they came in the end in their billions to the power of 10
to protect the machine
from the people who wouldn't stop yelling
work, yes, but let it be fair!

work, yes, but let it be fair!

a little part of it

there was this keypad in front of him
all of the alphabet and all of the numbers printed on it
there was a wire that led from it that went into this box
and when he pressed its buttons, the box digested it
before chucking them out as instructions
other people many miles away received them
and they followed his instructions, went to addresses and picked
    up parcels
then went to the top of the hill to deliver them

the keypad became his tool
the wire his veins
the box his heart

and this was just his keypad, his wire, that went into his box
which was just the littlest part of it

the slide

they say there soon won't be any jobs left
that they'll all be done by machines
or some other associated technology
they say that Michael from accounts
won't be able to moan anymore
while in the lunch room eating his falafels
about the extra hours he has to do
when the end of month invoices need getting out
they say that Maria the cleaner
won't be able to be happy anymore
as she goes around the office
whistling and humming to the Taylor Swift songs playing in her
    earphones
because there won't be an office
where workers will sit and make it dirty
for Maria's happiness to be needed
they say that Roman the mechanic
won't be able to pump his fists up into the air anymore
around the workshop after his Friday shift finishes
after he's healed 4 more bikes and 3 more vans which were close
    to death
so that they could get back out on the road
earning more money for the couriers and The Man
they say that Carlos's hands and the instep of his right foot
    might not even be needed
as he clicks into gear and turns the revs to shoot his motorbike
    through the streets of London
avoiding death by millimetres at least twenty times a day
with magic in his heart and instinct in his guts
picking up documents and bags of blood
only to deliver them safely into soft hands

but I'm not having any of that
because if that does happen
what will all the people do?
where will all the people go?

the Sophie principle

Sophie knew what was what
she worked on our Track & Trace desk
monitoring the Major client's jobs
letting them know when something was delayed
or was about to go seriously wrong
but whenever it got too busy
without anyone noticing her looking around for some help or
    support
her anxiety would kick in
and she had two big bottomless eyes
like something deep that knew the sea
and you could sense that she was softer than an octopus
only twice as wise
that she'd learned to grow three hearts
one for working one for living and one for her anxiety
while the others in there were shark-cold with their metals and steel
while she was all warm and flesh and caring
with the children still to come

they say aliens are out there somewhere
that when they come, they will bring us a different knowledge
but fuck that
if we had 10 Sophies with all that blood and spirit clashing about
    inside them
that would be enough for me
that would even be enough I reckon
to convince all of the scientists to turn their telescopes around
and begin to start examining
how much more beautiful and rich we are than the stars

Deshane Jackson

there wasn't anywhere else for her to run to
no scholarship or internship she could afford
to attend while rent and food had its clamps
clasped around her winged ankles

I told her
this is the only internship or scholarship you need
to learn what it is like
to be used by the machine
she looked at me back like I was a minister
who her whole life had been finger-wagging at her

when she got the job she told me
that there was a celebration called in the old flat
a Sunday afternoon where mum cooked more than a herd could eat
and uncles and aunts came around
to slap her on the back and toast her

when the email came in from the client praising her
for the way she'd diligently and patiently dealt with their problem
she was voted 'new star' of the month
and given a £20 Sainsbury's voucher

a bit of unleaded
pumped into the insides of the machine
can sometimes lessen the effects of rust
felt in the throat and stomach of a veteran

tears can well
the heart beats a little bit faster
and once again
you can feel optimism begin to stir in your blood
hearing the clank and clunk of the machine stutter
from such purity being fed into it

the unsaid

he worked there for 8 years
in the accounts department one floor up from me
and I think I only spoke to him twice
once when we were in the kitchen trying to work out if it was me
or him first
to use the microwave
'you go ahead' he said
'thank you' I said back
and then the other time was tonight 3 years after he'd left
I was rushing home from Paddington station in the rain
and he was coming the other way
we bumped into each other on the steel steps bridge beside the
fish restaurant barge that sells oysters
he had his hood up and I had my umbrella open
both of our heads were down
and we sort of bumped into each other
and as it happened he looked at me and knew
and I looked at him and knew
'you go ahead' I said
'thank you' he said
10 words in 11 years
which was more than enough
for both of us to know
almost everything

the flaw

I knew it was you when the heavens shook
not since the last time has any creature reached up high enough
to rattle the steel of my chambers
you found the way in between the beauty of acorn to oak
such mystery must be peered into
sliced open then dissected
and there you found it
a mirror held up to your gleaming cities
it is my fault
not one thing I have made without flaw
set to spring its trap when you come upon it
no warning signs are there
but for the instinct I planted in your gene
that you cut free
dashed into the boiling sea
and replaced with your machine language

descent

first there was everything
before it all started to subside towards nothing
first there were the trees and the birds sitting in them
singing even louder
and your rivers ran as though with the blood of a million
    legionaries
until they became congealed with your advancement
then someone said
is this all that we have left of it
and it reverberated around the cities and the mountains
but no one heeded anything
this was all that you had left
in your parked cars in your own waiting
unable to look back
at the landscape of burnt stumps
behind you

you are ill Adam

ill with the inhalation of smoke
stoked from the flames and furnaces
that line the cramped lanes
your families bend the knee to now
I didn't see the machines, the wires
that would replace my veins
coming to pump a different blood around you
I didn't see them taking over
I just sat in your heart stupid as a wave
that the sea kept giving
Adam, there's no need to look for me anymore
I am no longer there
you have replaced me
the wind that stood your hair up on the long walk to St Trudo's
up on to the top of the Great Orme
where the Earth's elbows crack against my cheek
that is not me anymore
I am at the bottom of that sea, tied to its bed
by some great iron instrument

the wind moves through the forgotten chapel eerily -
who knows where the next altars will be built for me
or even if they will

progress

it's not that you who were constantly tired or asleep
missed something
though guilt always comes back in hindsight to haunt
it was more like the machine's components needed no rest
and worked their way to ascend you

first they ate away at the paraphernalia
the ticket and the 2nd conductor
and when they became a distant memory
they set their metals at the rebuilding of the city
eating through the stock of once bearable homes
until there was nothing left
but the bricks and mortar stuck like little fishbones
between their iron teeth

and then the chip and the algorithms came
software implanted after the second wave
dressed up like fairy tales you preferred to the first versions
leaving your blood and bones behind
in that different country
for the new one
full of gold and avatars
you could reset or change at will

when the next stage comes it will probably
implant itself in your wrist
when all I ever wanted was for you to offer yourself to me
talk to me in the stone chapel
or somewhere else you felt more comfortable with
between the first breath and the last screams
of your hideous progress

defeat

I gave you a larger cranium to grow
and what did you go and do with it
you filled it with the puss of your progress
why couldn't you stop at the painting
the drawings on your cave walls
were the magic of the plants
not enough to ink yourself into the world with
you were given the world in the perspective of an Adam & Eve
a Punch & Judy
you took that and went and invented the oil rig
the property market, borders
now you tie telescopes to your eyes
yet you can't see further than your newly acquired genitals
you tie microscopes to your eyes
yet you do nothing about the division between the cells of an
employer and employee
you put bears inside cages then let song contests define how you feel
some of you have even tried to buy a fucking star
how many times do I need to try
to second guess your blood's whisperings
will the same way the grandmother loved her old land
never be enough for you

camping for two nights under a tree at Enfield Lock

what does this land have to do
with the men he works next to each day
only that without them
there would be no root for this tree
to grow above their harshness
or for a bird to come on the sunrise
to twirl its song into his ear
helping him up eager
to get over the fields of yet another day

in the city, it is just over there, it is worse
there is no song no fields no birds
but for the scavengers
and their poems mirror that, there is no
beauty in them, other than the machines' well-oiled roar
and roars they say are their truth, but

catch one
by the waterlogged field on a lazy spring night
when the scent shares its different language
watch that one's nose twitch and sniff at it
trying to decipher it
then watch it slowly succumb
to moonbeam and the beating sac
of the land like a new-born
as though the city and its machines
didn't even exist

graffiti found on the side of a church in Enfield

if the future is our demise
and the past was our potential
does that mean there was somewhere in between the two
when we had the chance to choose?

and because we are where we are now
does that mean that we didn't choose well?

the turning

the people started to wonder
if they'd come this far
and built all of this
out of just earth and mud
it couldn't be down to just chance
could it?

surely they were special
something bigger than themselves
something bigger than their wars
something bigger than their toothache

but why then the pain
why the struggle
why the dislocation of the heart from the mind
why the introduction of such complicated love
why should it be either the bee or intensive farming
why couldn't it be both
where was the freedom where was the joy
what was it meant exactly by compromise
surely that wasn't something they had to deal with
was it?

and sure enough
slowly they turned from being people
into becoming creatures

the blood

she sat on the skull of Hercules
staring into the eyes of Medusa
wondering what else in this galaxy of hers she had to do
to tip them off that they'd taken a wrong turn

why was it
every gift she gave them
they turned into a problem
every offering she yielded them
they eat to the bone until nothing was left
every animal she introduced to them
they caged or hunted to the brink of extinction

she looked at the blueprints of their heart again
it all looked fine
the atria and ventricles didn't seem to have any inherent fault
blood would come in and then blood would pump out

then it suddenly hit her
like a meteor in between the eyes
it was in the blood!
because everything else
the ribcage the cheekbones the pelvis
the liver the lips the fingernails
she'd overseen the construction of
checked it all 4 billion times
before finally letting it loose to grow out of the earth and mud

only the blood and plasma she'd gotten from him
it was the only thing that'd bring then keep them alive
everything else she'd made on her own
to utter perfection
it was the blood and plasma she just new it
and that bastard owned every last drop of it

the Inventor

the Inventor said
if you know better
go, do more then
and the creature tried
but with its ankles and wrists
already broken from his machines' spools
the creature managed only 4 steps
before it fell over and built a church
so that all of the other creatures
could come and worship along with him
their invalidity
under a sign they'd hung up on its door

the Inventor's House it said

widening the divide

the Inventor asked
who is it you worship?
the creatures replied
love money and rage

the Inventor asked
who is it that feeds you and keeps you warm of a night?
the creatures replied
your brutality, your metal teeth and our mothers
the sweat and guile of them

the Inventor asked
isn't it my machinery that has created everything?
the creatures replied, yes, yes, we are chained

the Inventor asked
so why don't you worship me then rather than your mothers?
the creatures replied
we're not sure why either
but it's got something to do with her flesh
the soothing nature of it when placed against our skin
and the warmth of her blood
when it's not being spilled or used against us

the Inventor knew then
that he hadn't quite cracked it
that something else was needed
to help widen that divide

watch me destroy all of that

let them suffer
let them come to me
with their rent problems and their electricity bills and their
damp
on the bedroom walls of their children
I will cause all of that the Inventor said
and also malnutrition and the loss of self-respect in their need
for survival
I will create food banks and division
and watch them drink up my oils
watch them bring more of their hands into my factories and
building sites
to help build more of my poison
watch them come tough as bears
only for me to break their backs
watch them try to bring up their young on fairy tales and songs
then watch me destroy all of that

the Inventor creates a device

the Inventor thought

this is coming along nicely
they are putting bears in cages
writing songs about suicide
they have become ugly and ripe
all they need is a little more help
and I will be 'this close'
to colonising them all

so he set about creating a device
made of metals rather than blood
and the creatures surprised him
because they instantly wanted more of his metals
rather than more of the warmth of each other's blood

this is the game changer

the Inventor thought
because even though it wasn't real
like the old church
they came to his new church online
donating more money per month than they'd ever done
and their children suddenly fell quiet
turned in on themselves
peering into their filthy nests
rather than out
then the device all of a sudden turned everything into a market
    square
and there were terrible arguments
about what she said and what he said
about what was right and what was wrong
and it was all done on a platform the Inventor had helped them build

like when Joan of Arc got burnt
truth and lies became almost indistinguishable
both a spear laced with venom thrown into a billion hearts at once
and no one could work out who was dead or who was dying
but bears were still being put in cages
and until that stopped
the Inventor's device was winning

the creatures were unhappy

politics had betrayed them
family had left them bereft and exhausted
the energy bill and council tax bill
both had their long pointed nails
tapping away all night at the glass panes of their bedroom
    windows
so when the machine came
offering itself in the form of a device -
all those apps all that connectivity all those platforms -
they gave away their integrity
and they gave it away happily with their smiley faces
with their cartoon hearts & fist-bump emojis
and the machine thought

I'm onto something here
they are stupider than I thought
let's have some fun

and their autonomy
suddenly became a stolen chariot on autopilot
and their love suddenly became
everything in the coliseum that wore the same colours as them
and their freedom
felt more real than before even though it'd diminished
and sex was just a swipe away
and rage and hope were fuelled
by fake Caesar's
and when they looked in the mirror of a night
while brushing their teeth
they could see what had happened to them
but they'd come this far already
so they took that nothing away with them to bed
and dreamt the Third Reich the slave trade the holocaust all over

again
and when they got up in the morning
they carried it around with them
like a lump
and the machine laughed
at how easy it'd been
as it kept on making more and more of itself

isolation

the last part of the trick
was getting them to believe
in something so outrageous so fundamental
that they couldn't see further than it
like love
like the rent needing to be paid
like tax codes hot water and the power of sport
and if you fed them well and cheaply enough
with sugars and fats
and if you centralised their media in the power of just six fists
all pushing the same precarious anxiousness of existence
it could work
and it would become a rare thing
for one to even dare lift their hand up above the rim of their nest
to seek another one's to hold
and before you knew it
they would all see themselves
as little spools and cogs
of a massive machine
too big and powerful for them to identify with
almost anything
other than their isolation

the creatures and the lopsided crown

there was detachment there was rage there was no long-term plan
burning its way through any of them

now-me! now-me! me-now!
shone through their eyes

this-moment-mine! this-moment-mine!
became the song for all of their tribes

and nothing became more important
than what they said
how they were perceived

it could've worked
but alive in each one of them
was only itself
the individual drama the individual struggle
and their groups became too small
and their gangs became too large
and every new day
was like 8 billion heads
raising themselves simultaneously above the filth of their nests
looking around for the next thing to eat
all opening their mouths at the same time
before squawking out into the air
this-moment-mine! this-moment-mine!

with a half-eaten worm
balanced on each one of their heads
like a lopsided crown

kissing

after all of the cities had been lost
after 92% of the creatures in them had been colonised
after internet connections had become more important than hearts
there was one thing left
too intimate and powerful to be shared randomly
but secretly done
like in an underground car park
where the hundreds of tons of concrete
suffocated the noise from outside
so that it all became a distant hum, a distant muffle in the ears
like you were both now in some kind of concrete womb
in which you could hear her breath actualy clash against yours
and where if nobody moved for three minutes
the lights would go out
leaving it completely black
so that none of the machine's eyes could see
and if you did it slowly
put your lips to her lips
so that your movement towards each other wouldn't trip its sensors
the importance of it
would light up everything

wanting to do it
became more important than anything
it was one of the last signs
you hadn't become one of them yet
but those who done it like it was a perfunctory act before sex
a question to answer on a job application
or with a force that couldn't be reckoned with
beaten back
they were the ones who'd dropped the ball
who were pretending
and lost

in some parts of the world
where the machines had completely taken over
doing it in the open
like in a market square
or on a public beach
or stealing one on a bench in the park
with a member of the same sex
could result in you either being decapitated
having one of your hands chopped off
or, at best
being sentenced to one year in prison

nothing was ever significant enough

I'll flash-flood 20,000 of them away
with one of my storms
I'll kill two and a half thousand of them in the centre of Morocco
with one of my earthquakes
while they are asleep in their beds
I'll spill sewage into their seas with my industry
I'll clog up their rivers with my wet wipes
I'll put
6 million of them on their NHS waiting list
for rudimentary procedures that could ease their pain
and then I'll make it 7, 8 million

but nothing would ever be significant enough

I'll make their football match tickets cost more than a week's worth
    of their wages
I'll destroy all of their little miracle's inter-school sport
I'll shut their libraries and their swimming pools down
and the bus routes
that connect their towns to their cities
I'll cancel
and I'll raise the price of eggs and beans
32% within 9 months
and then I'll tear their seabed to shreds
dragging them apart with 3 ton dragnets
pulled by 50 ton trawlers
that I'll help them create

but nothing would ever be significant enough

I'll give them food made in laboratories
I'll give them love online
I'll give them the art of the tattoo
and I'll watch them cover themselves
with their hopeless ink
and then I'll give them war
and the laser beam
and the two-headed dog
and the mutated fish
with its 4 eyes and one giant tooth
growing up out of the top of its head
and I'll make them pay for health care
tooth extractions
sex
and the price they'll have to pay for it
will be in their nightmares
and their pain will not even make it out of their own atmosphere
and their passing will be like a drop of water evaporating on a hot
    plate
and it will be well and good when they are gone

because nothing was ever significant enough for them

what to do with your freedom

the Inventor said
WAR!
who amongst you is willing to wage it?

no one answered
so the Inventor said again
WAR!
who amongst you is willing to throw the first stone?

again no one answered
so the Inventor said
why do you think I let you create all of your religions?
get on with it
you have been proved to be useless
let's have some fun

but again no one answered
so rather than asking over and over again
the Inventor set about hurrying up
the perfection of the satellite
its correct altitude the size of its wings
the mass manufacturing principle of white phosphorus
the way it can be made to fall beautiful as snow
only to land then burn away the skin
and the drone
uglier than a dragonfly
but perfected with it in mind
able to get up there above the clouds
firing off its missiles

WAR!
the Inventor said again

I created you for it
you creatures you cattle you factories of blood
what is wrong with you
I've given you everything you need

WAR!
the Inventor went on screaming it out
WAR!
WAR!
KILL HIM!
KILL THEM ALL!

and when everyone started to accept
that this must be the way
that this must be what they were made for
they suddenly became content
for they had lost the hardest part of themselves

which was what to do with their freedom

colonisation

some say
it wasn't the Inventor's fault
that it's all been a big mistake
a silly identification error

others say
that he doesn't even exist
that he's just a concept
dreamt up
by needy souls in a vast and lonely universe

and yet others say
that it was the creatures who first developed the machines
and because they couldn't then see far without a telescope
or close enough without a microscope
began using them against each other
thus starting off the process
of colonisation

and if you go back through their history books
you'll find little bits of truth
like dropped sweets forming a path
that will lead you to support or contradict
all of the above

and that's the thing about the creatures
their history is almost always personal
always banging on about what they can see on the surface
never about what's an inch underneath
never mind miles

a good pair of eyes

in the darkness they are more useful than light

the towns are set on fire constantly
it comes from the sky in a metal bird

corneas cannot stand too much heat, before they shrivel up
like flame dropped onto a piece of cling film

I come out some days
to find my neighbour feeling about in the bins

blindness is our only weapon, our only defence
the eyes refuse to see, they are too busy from being squeezed shut

no one knows precisely when this happened
only that it was around the time the wars started

one device can light up a whole neighbourhood
blind 8 billion creatures forever

on the front of the newspapers
they say more devices are coming

no one reads them anymore
no one can see anything very much

everything is too bright
in the darkness they are more useful than light

the screams of the supervisors

you can't always decipher what the screams of the supervisors mean
so numerous are they
sometimes they sound like moos from within a herd
drowned out by the rest of the heard
then other times they are like the beatings of a silverback's chest
charging into a clearing in the forest
before just standing there
looking for the surprise and shock to appear on all of our faces
so that it can make him feel hard and relevant again

sometimes they are like the bite of a hyena into the back of your
    neck
other times they are like the annoying whimpering of a chained-up
    dog
and sometimes they are as ferocious and directed as a snake bite
leaving you feeling anxious and nervous
from how much poison they might've injected into you
and yet other times
they are like the howl of a lonely wolf
howling at something unknown
unheard
alone

but mostly
they are like the coughing-up bark from some hideous animal
afflicted by a great disease
coming from somewhere far off
in the dense electronic wood

a cupcake cunt

supervisor Glyn is in a state
he's in a rage
because the client that has his number
as a point of contact
has called him up and is screaming at him
the van they've booked to take the cupcakes this client makes
is an hour late
and those cupcakes are now not going to make the deadline
so that they can be spread out on a white linen table
at the JP Morgan lunch time event

supervisor Glyn can't keep it in
he has saliva in both corners of his mouth
his heart is almost visibly beating through his £90 shirt
as he storms around the control room
trying to find the guilty controller
running around like a toddler who's had too much sugar
with his mobile at his ear
telling the cupcake making client on the other end
that he's going to sort it
that he's going to find the reason why this has happened
and remove it root and branch
so that it will never happen again

finally he finds the control point
where the guilty controller is sat
and he tells the cupcake making client
that he's found the problem
and will call them back in a sec

his neck now is all swollen
the veins in it are out
like his insides are about to become his outsides
and then he starts

you useless idiot!
what the fuck are you doing?
don't you know what's at stake here?
don't you know your job
your very existence
rests on you making all of this work
are you a moron or something?

the guilty controller tells him back
that it's been really busy
that he hasn't got enough vans
to cover all of the jobs
that keep dropping down onto his screen like confetti
supervisor Glyn is having none of it though
goes back at him with the bellows of his ugly lungs
ejecting more of their rancid vocabulary

the van finally picked up the cupcakes
and were delivered one hour and fifteen minutes late to the venue
none of us know if the cupcakes made the white linen table of the
    JP Morgan event
but we all knew what supervisor Glyn is

revenge fuck

after supervisor Glyn
had stormed into the control room
to rip the trainee controller apart
because he'd fucked up
and not got the JP Morgan banking job collected
so that the cheques could be deposited on time
causing JP Morgan to lose
more interest than what it costs to build a nuclear bomb

after supervisor Glyn
went in at that trainee controller
with his anger and his lust and his lost heart
ripping him apart like a lion
who'd found a little lame wildebeest at the watering hole
stripping it first of all of its skin
before crunch-breaking its bones

after supervisor Glyn
walked away telling that trainee controller
that his days were already numbered
with blood all over the collars of his £90 shirt
and saliva dripping from his ugly mouth
some of the other controllers decided to buy balaclavas
and find out where supervisor Glyn lived

none of them had planned it
but it sure felt good dragging supervisor Glyn by the collar of
    that £90 shirt
into a disused garage
somewhere up around Northolt
to do what they had to do
to put things right

the rule of the 4th floor

no one is sure where the rule came from
that we couldn't use the 4th floor
to go and eat our lunches

I mean, it was a perfectly good floor
with one long room
and a long table made of wood
that saw very little use
apart from when all the important people came
for their meetings

it was a shame
as there was a door that opened out onto a roof terrace
with big windows all along one side that let in the sky
making it look wider and bigger
than it looked through the little windows
in our designated lunch room

no one knows where the rule came from
that we weren't allowed to use the room on the 4th floor
to go and eat our lunches
or even to go on one of our breaks, to sit
and admire the sky

maybe it had something to do with sanctity
like you can't enter certain places in a church
unless you have first proved that you believe in the Inventor
or maybe it was about place
our lot knowing ours
and their lot keeping hold of theirs

it might even have been to prevent suicides
to stop people from taking a run up
before jumping off its edge
or it could've been
to stop people sitting in an open space for too long
so that daydreaming would begin
and a plan of escape
start to hatch

but there weren't any rumours about it
no whispers or stories from the past
it was just a rule
we had to obey

VAR

they said it would help
they said it would eradicate mistakes
they said it'd show up the fine lines
the play acting
the diving
for what they really were
millionaire ballerinas getting blown over
mid-pirouette
by the wind

they said
it would make everything more real and authentic
because it would reveal the truth

they said all the lies would be found out
that nothing would be unfair anymore
that everything would be judged now
by centimetres, millimetres
with impartiality
so there could never be another mistake

when in reality
it was just another device
that would take even more beauty and chance
away from this world
than already had been

then, on the day it was to be introduced
from the darkness
out stepped a creature into the light
huffing and puffing like a big beast
with sweat on its brow and a club in its hand
and announced

I shall interpret its images
I shall calculate all possibilities
I shall ignore all allegiances
then I shall share with you the truth

and this was just one creature who lied

skinjobs

at one point
after they'd recognised the Inventor's hand
but before he'd perfected his machines
there must've been this time
when they lived not too much in brute ignorance
but neither blindfolded by arrogant incompetence either

there must've been this time
however fleeting
when they entered into the centre of the hurricane
and all was perfectly in balance
behind them the butchery and senseless burnings
in front of them Taylor Swift and the power of the split atom

that time
when instinct still had its own room in their heads
and dominated
rather than now
with these warehouses
stuffed full of components
for these poisonous machines

who needs a Socrates when there's only one bee left

after all of the cities had been taught their lesson
and all of the creatures in them had been occupied
one wood remained
still thick with trees
somewhere near Uxbridge
and even though there were no butterflies
or foxes left
a leaf fell from an oak
to the floor
and underneath it
the last bee left
sat trembling with fear
knowing that its job
was to go out there and find honey

less arms more bees

the people were important
but only up to a point
there was always something going on with them
always some kind of drama
some kind of disaster
some kind of vial containing some kind of wrong colour blood

bees on the other hand
there was nothing to discuss
they needed to be kept alive
even if that meant putting your arm
into one of their engines
that kept one of their factories alive
so that it would shut it down
and nobody could eat energy for two days

then if another person put their arm in
on the 3rd day
then another person
on the 6th day
then another
on the 9th

and if this kept going on and on like love
like a drama
like if we didn't do it then we would face disaster
and nobody could eat
anything anymore other than honey
or hear
anything else above the buzz and drone from the billions of bees
now lifting off from the meadows
then that would be better
than this

a reproductive system

there wasn't one
or ten
but billions of them
convinced that something else existed
other than them

it wasn't known why
but some of them tried to guess
while sitting on the lap of a priest
or on their knees in between an imam's thighs
with the favourite being
how could we have let this be done
to ourselves?
no other creature on Earth
has shown such servile stupidity
surely this is proof
of the Inventor's interference
and his loathing of us?

and it was an awful itching urge
that'd been buried deep in the centre of them
that wanted to bring more of them into the world
to see if they also agreed

impulse

we were walking along the canal towards the zoo
then on towards Camden Market for chips in a cone
when under the bridge by Prince Albert Road
a stickleback fat as a sardine
suddenly leapt out of the water and landed in front of us
we all stopped in shock
as we watched it slapping itself against the concrete
then all of a sudden the girl broke free from her mother's hand
took three 5-year-old strides
and stamped on it
the blood of it squirted up all over her little legs
there were bits of it in between her tiny toes
and then she started to cry
her mother looked at me
and I looked at her back
both of us knowing
that the machines were gonna have trouble taming this one

peering over the precipice

when the children dropped off the breast
when they had to start navigating rather than being led
when they realised
that it was now that they had to stop believing in all the stories
    and lies

they said, 'mum, dad,
what have you done?'

learning

to unlearn
to unlearn the need for food for heat
to unlearn the cold night
for the sun to rise and make it yet another day
to unlearn the entrance into the tube system
so that you can get at your job
feeling like a carcass electrocuted alive by the alarm clock
to sit on one of their trains
a quarter of a mile under their city
shooting through the bones and mud
taking you to another 10 hour shift
where all of the supervisors think they are in charge of Rome
who will inspect your performance stats
like they used to inspect the teeth of slaves on a platform in the
    Campo de' Fiori
to see if they were healthy enough to keep
3 fails, and you're off to the Colosseum
to queue in a line for tins
to queue in a line for sanitary products
to queue in a line fat on carbs and welfare cash
to queue in line one after the other after the other
for life for survival for what?

to learn
to learn how to steal from those who need to be stolen from
Tesco's Sainsbury's TfL
Waitrose John Lewis British Gas
and for when it gets too unbearable
to learn how to sit in the dark drinking dark
to learn how to use yourself
you are a piece of meat
you are a cow a sheep a bull a hooved thing

learn
it will never get better
it will always get worse

the season ticket holders will not believe in you
the editors and politicians will not believe in you
and sometimes
your woman will not believe in you either

our guts

our guts work like engines
they are embedded deep inside us
our guts can hold their breath
they sit sniper-still for days months
their fingers are not our fingers
that tap away at keypads all day
trying to make it happen trying to make it
all seem okay
they have been decapitated from them

our guts shower in fire they kiss in smoke
they live in a little pit inside the centre of us
when they talk to you
and you can't do what they say
they get upset
you have to listen to them
you have to try

they are the most important part of us
they are the only things left
that we can bring to the table

we talk to them at night...

where were you today?
why'd you go missing on me like that
when that supervisor gave me that bollocking?
why didn't you rise then
send all these words you're now sending me
into my mouth
so I could've told him...

they never speak back
they are too tired from being ignored

our guts work like engines
they are embedded deep inside us
you gotta talk to them
ask them questions
asking them questions
will light up the way
or at least let you know
that you haven't got any

and if you haven't got any
hold their imaginary hand
on dark evenings filled with rain
when there is lightning in the air
and tanks circling the outskirts of your city

they will come back to you

you may not have it in you now to use them
but they will always be there

they will always be there

and one day
they will reward you
and everything will feel
almost okay

Enoch's hammer

the HR meeting had been brutal
all 6 warehousemen had been called
to listen to the bitches in bearskins and beards
explain how now that the new Inventory Management System
   had been installed
and been proved to be more than efficient
somewhere centrally invisibly keeping tabs on all of the stock
before automatically firing off fulfilment orders to the vendors
who'd then deliver in the new parts within 24 hours
there wouldn't be the need for all 6 warehousemen anymore
to spend pointless costly hours
manually collating all of the picked and packed parts
onto a spreadsheet
before attaching them to emails and pressing buttons
so each of the vendors knew what they had to replace

the businesses needs had changed the dragon said
and unfortunately
all of you are being put on notice
but it wasn't over just yet
because all 6 of you will be able to apply
for the 4 jobs that remain

that was on Thursday
on Saturday afternoon
one of the men was working a midday to 10pm shift
and when an order came in to pick a part
the new software let out its siren
and the bay and shelf number
printed a ticket

the part was on the 2nd floor
one floor down
where the lights weren't so bright
and the CCTV wasn't so covering
so he put the hammer in his pocket
and got into the lift

at the terminal
he lifted the barcode scanner out of its charging socket
and rather than going to pick the part
he placed the scanner on the floor
got the hammer out of his pocket
and began smashing it to pieces

then he turned back to face the terminal
it's keyboard and big 28 inch monitor...
the first crack shot all the button casings of the keypad up into
    the air
then the second one
splintered it apart
and then the third
aimed straight into the centre of the monitor
smashed its screen
leaving it all indigo and blue

then underneath the desk
where the computer tower
housing all of its evil hid
he pulled it out
and placed it in front of him
it took 4 cracks
to break its casing
then 8 more
to destroy all of the components inside

he looked around at all of the stock
and for one minute
he thought about it
but it wasn't their fault he reasoned
everyone needs bits and bobs to keep their lives going
it's the way they're now being looked after that was the problem
so he decided not to
walked off to get back in the lift up to the 3rd floor
where his coat and rucksack were waiting

he wasn't going to bother
applying for one of the 4 jobs that remained
he already had the taste in his mouth about what needed to be done
was off to the big Sainsbury's off Whitechapel Rd
where there were only 3 checkouts left
that still had humans behind tills
to see what his hammer could achieve there
at the self-checkout terminals...

it was a Saturday morning

after another one of their brutal weeks
the lady was across the road getting her coffee
while he was in Tesco's trying to buy a can of gin
he scanned it at the self-checkout
and the words came out
telling him he'd have to wait for assistance to verify his age
one minute went by
before he started looking around
there were customer's everywhere
prodding their melons feeling their avocados
and the one lady behind the counter
was busy scanning a big shop
with eight more in line
so he let another minute go by
hearing her ring the bell for support
then another minute went by
he could see through the big glass windows
cars going by and people walking their dogs
and it wasn't until the 5th minute until he snapped
started to try and pull the chip and pin machine out of its holder
it took four tugs of it to break it free
and then when it did there were wires dangling out of the end of
it like veins
and now he'd done it it felt like a grenade in his hands that was
about to go off
so he chucked it on the floor and began stamping on it
and a guy in the queue way behind him said
'go on brother, kill it'
so he killed it with his weekend boots
and then he used the back of the can of his gin
to smash the screen in front of him telling him that assistance
was coming
then all of a sudden

three people with Tesco badges on their chests came
and he said
'ah, you're here now, where were you when I needed you to
verify my age?'
but they didn't answer him, they just looked at him and said
'we will call the police'
then the man in the queue who'd given him some
encouragement
chucked a packet of tomatoes at them
but he said
'hold on, it's not their fault, it's the CEOs and entrepreneurs who
introduced these machines
so that they could swipe away the cost of staff from
their spreadsheets'
'yes', the man in the queue said, 'you are quite right, sorry
brothers'
then a woman who was wearing a red coat and had a dog
in a handbag said
'I don't know why this hasn't happened sooner'
then another man, behind the man in the queue who'd given the
first man some encouragement said
'there's another terminal there next to you – smash that one with
your can of gin too'
so the man smashed that one with the back of his can of gin
and the people wearing the badges said
'we will call the police'
then a little lady, wee as the stem of a lily, came up to him
with just a packet of Tilda rice in her hands
and asked him if he could hurry up
because she needed to get back to feed her dog
so the man made way for her so that she could get by
to try and scan to pay for her rice
and on the way out
he thought about smashing the three screens of
the three terminals left
but he suddenly became frightened
because if he did that then it might never stop

where would it end?
so he walked out and went back to the lady across the road
who was drinking her coffee
and then the man in the coffee shop said
'sorry, but you're not allowed to drink gin in here...'

the artefact

in the early days
before the machines had been perfected
the people knew that they had to reboot
on a Sunday afternoon between 2 and 4pm
that their eyes then would be closed
while they dreamt to repair their awful organs

the freedom in those two hours
were used to mend things that had been ordered to
remain broken
to break eggs and make an omelette
to do pirouettes on a pinhead
or for each household
to peel back once again the corner of their plastic mat
removing the steel slats in the floor
under which the felt package was hid
grasping it then, in the dark scooping up of their hands
before carefully lifting it and ferrying it to the table
where they'd lay it down gently unwrapping it
to reveal in its felts' soft nuzzled insides
that old, banned now, artefact

the people would then take turns
for each to pick it up and hold it, grip it
to feel it again, imagine it
wood!
almost slippery with a black grain and a slight curve
that seemed to buzz when laid across the skin of a palm
feel it again, the Elder's would say
how it once could've been part of a hammer, or an axe
a chisel or a lever
how it could've been part of a handle to a giant door
that you could grip, open it
to go somewhere else that's now been lost
to the metals the machines prefer

then at 3.55pm
the artefact would be carefully wrapped up
and gently put back
before the machines woke up
and stopped everything from feeling almost real again

what resistance means

it first bores itself into you when you are younger
the type of music you listen to
that catches you on your own
18 and naked inside your bedroom
air-guitaring in front of the mirror

next
some catastrophic event
will shatter you

then as you get a bit older
you will learn to compartmentalise that
then the loneliness will kick in
and you will sleep under the iron moon
dreaming ugly dreams

then when you get your first job
it will be there
crystallising inside your fingertips
tapping away at their buttons
trying to make it all feel okay
trying to make it all seem fine
then when you take those fingertips home with you
it will hurt

if it doesn't hurt then you haven't got it
and you will never know what it means

later
your voice will become hoarse from constantly trying to
speak for it
your heart will become scarred and miss the occasional pump
from constantly trying to fight for it
your lungs will become black and your liver bloated
from the nights when you smoked and drunk to it

then even later
when you are on your own in the dark wood of sleep
you will meet it
and you will nod to it
and if it passes you by without nodding back
you will know that its appearance at least meant you came close
but that your soul wasn't strong enough
this time to change anything
but that next time it could

hope

there was this one thing
that couldn't be colonised

the creatures couldn't put their finger
on what it was

it wasn't the colour of their skin
it wasn't the shape of their genitals
it wasn't how much they were being underrepresented

and though they went to work each day
and used the machine's money
to pay their rent their council tax
their food their water their heat
at the end of the day
there was this one thing that remained
that wasn't the machines

it wasn't the happiness of fools
it wasn't the romanticism of poets
it wasn't even the knowledge
that they were made up of blood and bone

no one could work out exactly what it was
but while it lasted
the machines could war over their elections and territories
as much as they wanted

because all the creatures needed
was a little bit of it
in a song in a poem in a kiss
and that would be enough
to keep them going until the next month

hope 2

what happens when there's none left
what happens when it's completely gone
what happens when you don't even realise
that you've stopped looking around for it
what happens when it has been replaced
by contented indifference
what happens when all the things that create it
like a kiss
like a poem
like a song
have been banned
or turned into subjects of non-interest
what happens
if only one of the things above happen

what happens then

museum visit

taken from Stuart O. Anderson & Shaun Slifer / Mattress Factory

the toolhead sits alone
in a room kept dark except for a single spotlight on the case that
now houses it
it is treated as a relic of a time other than our own
its power must be feared
otherwise
why would it be kept in this plexiglass case
guarded by security cameras on each wall
and a proximity-triggered alarm?

treating this former implement of rebellion
safe now in a plexiglass box in a quiet and guarded museum
as a piece of art –
the toolhead itself
vibrates still –
it's as though they think its power has been contained
against any future inspiration or use
but they are wrong

because he took a picture of it
and tomorrow he will share it with his kid
who later will tell her kid
about how stupid her dad is
travelling 6 hours there and back
on a £79 return ticket
when there's little food in the fridge
just so he could see and feel what it was like
to be around a toolhead
that once smashed itself into the first machines
wondering the whole way home
how big and strong those first men and women must've been

just to be able to lift that
toolhead up into the air

the definition of what's not a machine

when the curve of her back means more to you than anything
when a tree
or a group of trees
like a wood or a forest
stand for something
when you want to kill something
like a politician or a bailiff or a traffic warden
but use reason not to
when you have a trinket or an artefact
left behind by the dead
that means something to you
immeasurably more than its appearance
when animals become your neighbours
rather than your trophies
when stars remain a mystery
rather than a solvable puzzle
when after eating beetroot
your pee comes out red
and you daydream for hours
about how everything is connected
when you can measure
evil or good
by the instinct inside your guts
rather than by a calculation
when there is an urge an urgency
in the things that you do
because you know that one day you will die

Acknowledgements

Some of these poems first appeared in the pamphlet *Machine Language* published by Culture Matters in 2023.

I would also like to thank Peter Raynard and Claire Jefferson for their guidance and editing skills when it all got a bit jumbled up and confusing.